THE CARPENTER
LESSONS ON CHARACTER BUILDING

THE NAMES OF CHRIST ILLUSTRATED
ACTIVITY BOOK

THE NOC ILLUSTRATED ACTIVITY BOOKS: AN AMAZING WAY TO TEACH YOUTH THE MANY DIFFERENT CHARACTERS OF CHRIST FOUND IN THE HOLY SCRIPTURES.

ISBN: 1-441-46170-1

PRINTED IN THE UNITED STATES OF AMERICA

COVER PAGE DESIGNED BY DYNAMIC ANIMATION PRODUCTIONS, LLC

PREFACE

"THE CARPENTER STRETCHETH OUT HIS RULE; HE MARKETH IT OUT WITH A LINE; HE FITTETH IT WITH PLANES, AND HE MARKETH IT OUT WITH THE COMPASS, AND MAKETH IT AFTER THE FIGURE OF A MAN, ACCORDING TO THE BEAUTY OF A MAN; THAT IT MAY REMAIN IN THE HOUSE."
ISAIAH 44:13 (KJV)

TO OUR PARENTS, TEACHERS AND GUARDIANS: IT IS A PRIVILEGE TO STUDY GOD'S WORD WITH YOUR CHILDREN AND A BLESSING TO TRAIN AND DISCIPLINE THEM FOR SERVICE IN THE MASTER'S CAUSE. ALONG WITH THEIR BIBLES, WE STRONGLY ENCOURAGE YOUR PARTICIPATION IN THE CHILD'S USAGE OF THIS ACTIVITY BOOK.

SECRET MESSAGE 1

A	B	C	D	E	F	G	H	I	J	K	L	M	N	O	P	Q	R	S	T	U	V	W	X	Y	Z
9	4	15	21	26	10	18	5	16	1	13	6	23	8	2	14	24	11	3	17	25	7	19	12	20	22

USE THE ABOVE KEYS TO DECODE THE MESSAGE BELOW

T H O U   H A S T   A L S O
17 5 2 25   5 9 3 17   9 6 3 2

G I V E N   M E   T H E
18 16 7 26 8   23 26   17 5 26

S H I E L D   O F   T H Y
3 5 16 26 6 21   2 10   17 5 20

S A L V A T I O N :   A N D
3 9 6 7 9 17 16 2 8 :   9 8 21

T H Y   G E N T L E N E S S
17 5 20   18 26 8 17 6 26 8 26 3 3

H A T H   M A D E   M E
5 9 17 5   23 9 21 26   23 26

G R E A T .
18 11 26 9 17 .

WHERE IS THIS TEXT FOUND: _____

SECRET MESSAGE 1: ANSWERS FOUND ON PAGE 37

UNSCRAMBLE EXERCISE
UNSCRAMBLE THE CHARACTER BUILDING WORDS BELOW

ACEORGU _____

DTTTEAUI _____

SPREETC _____

UVSLAE _____

PGCANITEC _____

ITDADEECD _____

WARKHODR _____

SRNAMEN _____

NYIUT _____

HRUTT _____

UNSCRAMBLE EXERCISE: ANSWERS FOUND ON PAGE 37

FILL IN THE BLANK
COMMIT THESE VERSES OF SCRIPTURE TO MEMORY

AND IN THE _____ MONTH THE ANGEL _____ WAS SENT FROM _____ UNTO A CITY OF _____, NAMED _____, TO A _____ ESPOUSED TO A MAN WHOSE _____ WAS _____, OF THE HOUSE OF _____; AND THE _____ NAME WAS _____. ~ LUKE 1:26,27

AND _____ SENT AND _____ AFTER THE _____. AND _____ SAID, IS NOT THIS _____, THE _____ OF _____, THE _____ OF _____ THE HITTITE? ~ 2 SAMUEL 11:3

AND _____ SAID UNTO _____, _____ ME NOT _____, CALL ME _____: FOR THE _____ HATH DEALT VERY _____ WITH ME. ~ RUTH 1:20

AND _____ SAID TO _____, TELL ME, I _____ THEE, _____ THY GREAT STRENGTH _____, AND _____ THOU _____ BE BOUND TO _____ THEE. ~ JUDGES 16:6

THEN _____ JESUS FROM _____ TO _____ UNTO _____, TO BE _____ OF HIM. ~ MATTHEW 3:13

AND _____ TALKED WITH _____ HIS _____: AND IT CAME TO PASS, WHEN THEY WERE IN THE _____, THAT _____ ROSE UP AGAINST _____ HIS _____, AND _____ HIM. ~ GENESIS 4:8

NOW THE LORD HAD _____ A GREAT _____ TO _____ UP _____. AND _____ WAS IN THE _____ OF THE FISH _____ DAYS AND _____ NIGHTS. ~ JONAH 1:17

AND ALL THE DAYS OF _____ WERE _____ _____ _____ AND _____ YEARS: AND HE DIED. ~ GENESIS 5:27

THEN SAID _____ UNTO _____, LORD, IF THOU _____ BEEN HERE, MY _____ HAD NOT _____. ~ JOHN 11:21

BUT _____ FOUND _____ IN THE _____ OF THE LORD. ~ GENESIS 6:8

3

"NAVIGATION IS KEY IN THE WORD OF GOD"

SEEK AND FIND YOUR WAY THROUGH THE MAZE BELOW

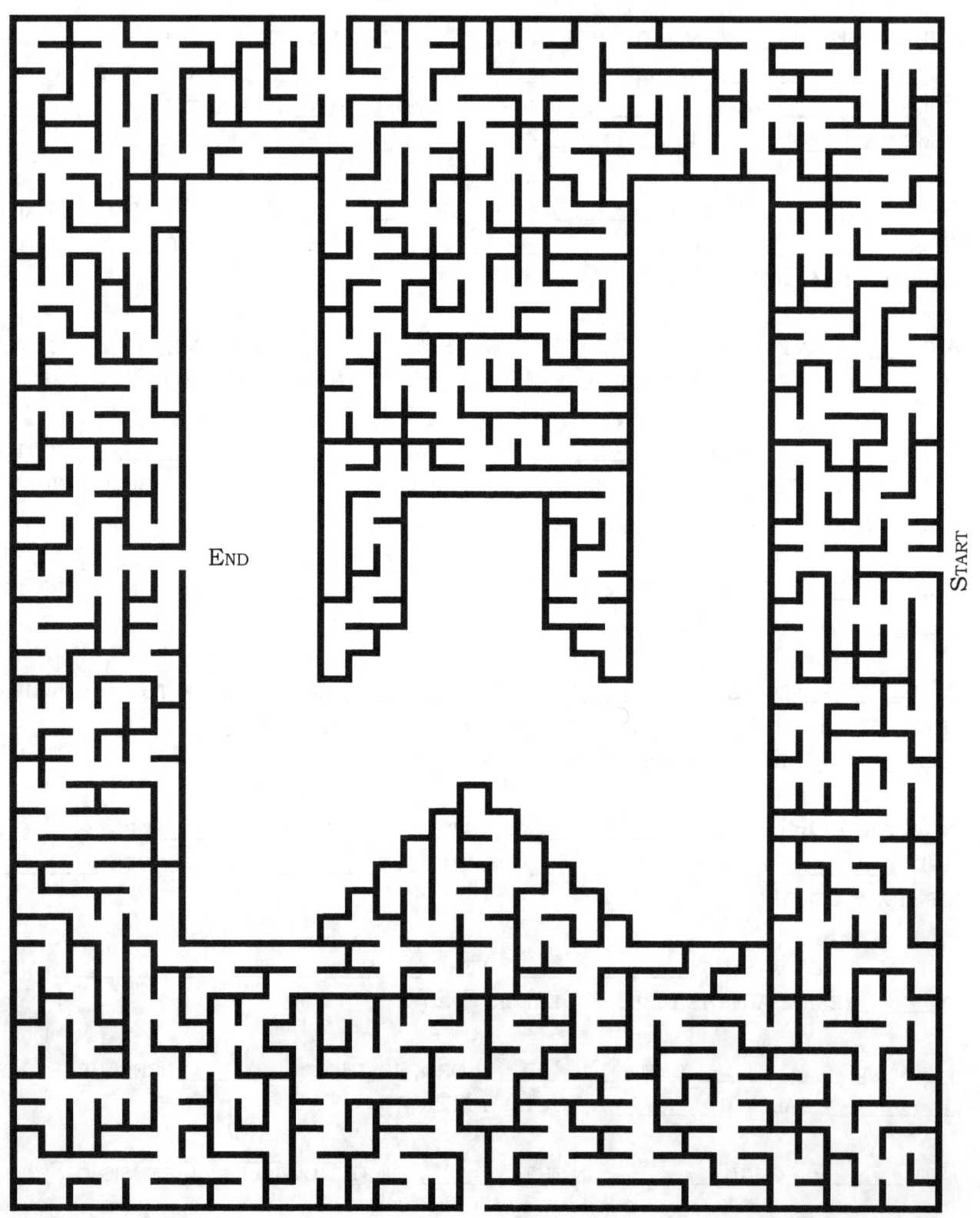

WONDERFUL WORDS OF LIFE
CROSSWORD PUZZLE 1

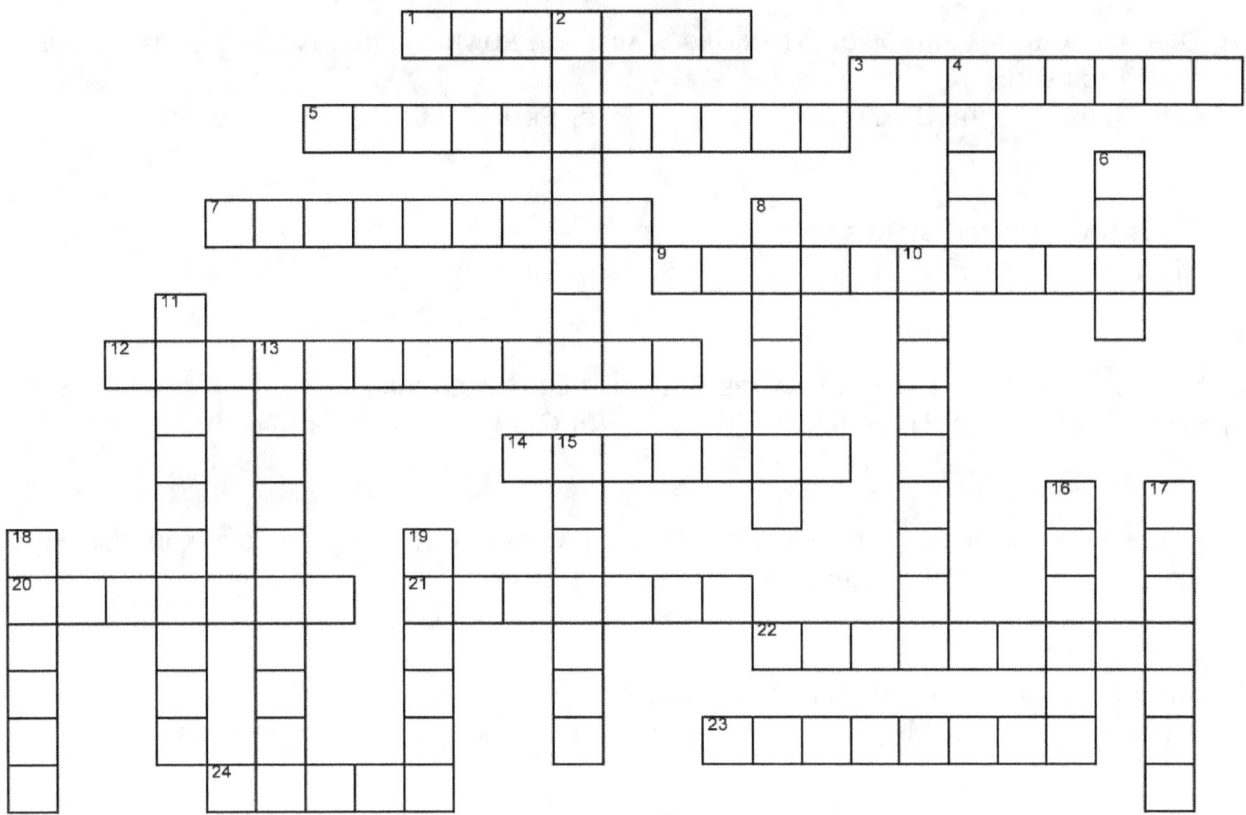

ACROSS

1. TO ESTEEM AS POSSESSED OF REAL WORTH. TO FEEL OR SHOW SPECIAL REGARD FOR.

3. ANY ACT OF BENEVOLENCE WHICH PROMOTES THE HAPPINESS OR WELFARE OF OTHERS.

5. DILIGENT IN BUSINESS OR STUDY; CONSTANTLY, REGULARLY OR HABITUALLY OCCUPIED IN BUSINESS; OPPOSED TO SLOTHFUL AND IDLE.

7. TO SET APART FOR GOD OR FOR RELIGIOUS PURPOSES; CONSECRATE. GIVEN WHOLLY TO.

9. THE PARDON OF AN OFFENDER, BY WHICH HE IS CONSIDERED AND TREATED AS NOT GUILTY.

12. OF A MERCIFUL OR COMPASSIONATE NATURE. PLEASING MANNER.

14. THE SOCIALLY CORRECT WAY OF ACTING; ETIQUETTE. THE PREVAILING CUSTOMS, SOCIAL CONDUCT, AND NORMS OF A SPECIFIC SOCIETY, PERIOD, OR GROUP.

20. THE QUALITY OR STATE OF BEING ONE; SINGLENESS OR WHOLENESS.

21. A PERSONAL TRAIT, ESPECIALLY A CHARACTER TRAIT. ESSENTIAL CHARACTER; NATURE. CONDITION IN RELATION TO OTHERS.

22. TO OFFER TO GOD IN HOMAGE OR WORSHIP; TO DEVOTE WITH LOSS.

23. INCLINED TO GIVE WAY OR COMPLY; FLEXIBLE; SURRENDER.

24. THE STATE OR QUALITY OF BEING ONE; SINGLENESS. AGREEMENT.

DOWN

2. A CALM TEMPER WHICH BEARS EVILS WITHOUT MURMURING OR DISCONTENT. SELF-CONTROL.

4. HAVING OR SHOWING QUALITIES OF HIGH MORAL CHARACTER, SUCH AS COURAGE, GENEROSITY, OR HONOR. EXALTED, DIGNIFIED.

6. INFLUENCED BY A REGARD TO THE LAWS OF GOD; OR LIVING IN EXACT CONFORMITY TO THE DIVINE WILL. RIGHTEOUS.

8. COURAGE; HEROISM; UNDAUNTED SPIRIT.

10. A PERSON WHO PERFORMS OR OFFERS TO PERFORM A SERVICE VOLUNTARILY.

11. THAT QUALITY OF A PERSON BY WHICH HE DESERVES THE CONFIDENCE OF OTHERS; FIDELITY; FAITHFULNESS; HONESTY.

13. DEEP AWARENESS OF THE SUFFERING OF ANOTHER COUPLED WITH THE WISH TO RELIEVE IT.

15. THE QUALITY OF BEING ABLE TO DO SOMETHING, ESPECIALLY THE PHYSICAL, MENTAL, FINANCIAL, OR LEGAL POWER TO ACCOMPLISH SOMETHING.

16. A STRONG AFFECTION FOR; HAVING TENDER REGARD FOR. FOND; AFFECTIONATE.

17. AN UPRIGHT DISPOSITION; CANDOR; TRUTH; FRANK SINCERITY.

18. ONE WHO WORKS AT A PARTICULAR OCCUPATION OR ACTIVITY. A PERSON THAT LABORS.

19. THE STATE, QUALITY, OR IDEAL OF BEING JUST, IMPARTIAL, AND FAIR. SOMETHING THAT IS JUST, IMPARTIAL, AND FAIR.

CROSSWORD PUZZLE 1: ANSWERS FOUND ON PAGE 34

BIBLE TRIVIA 1: FAMOUS BIBLE CHARACTERS

1. THIS MAN WAS SICK AND DIED. WHEN JESUS ARRIVED, HOWEVER, HE IMMEDIATELY RAISED HIM FROM THE DEAD.
A) ZACCHAEUS   B) JONAH   C) PETER   D) LAZARUS

2. JESUS WAS BAPTIZED BY THIS MAN.
A) MATTHEW   B) PAUL   C) TIMOTHY   D) JOHN

3. SHE TOLD ALL TO CALL HER "MARA" BECAUSE OF HER DEPRESSION.
A) RUTH   B) HANNAH   C) ORPAH   D) NAOMI

4. KING DAVID COMMITTED THE INDIRECT MURDER OF URIAH BECAUSE OF HIS LOVE FOR HER.
A) DELILAH   B) BATHSHEBA   C) LEAH   D) ABIGAIL

5. SHE TOOK A MAN'S STRENGTH SIMPLY BY HAVING HIS HAIR CUT.
A) DELILAH   B) MARY   C) REBEKAH   D) DEBORAH

6. WHO WAS SWALLOWED BY A GREAT FISH?
A) JONAH   B) JUDAS   C) PETER   D) JOHN

7. HE WAS THE ONLY LIVING RIGHTEOUS MAN WHEN GOD SENT THE GREAT FLOOD.
A) JONAH   B) NOAH   C) ABRAHAM   D) ADAM

8. THIS ANGEL TOLD MARY THE NEWS ABOUT HER GIVING BIRTH TO THE MESSIAH.
A) GABRIEL   B) LUCIFER   C) GALADRIEL   D) IT WAS GOD

9. ACCORDING TO THE BIBLE, WHO WAS THE OLDEST MAN WHO EVER LIVED?
A) ABRAHAM   B) NOAH   C) ADAM   D) METHUSELAH

10. HE IS RECORDED AS COMMITTING THE FIRST MURDER IN THE BIBLE.
A) CAIN   B) ADAM   C) MOSES   D) ABEL

BIBLE TRIVIA 1: ANSWERS FOUND ON PAGE 36

COLORING ACTIVITY

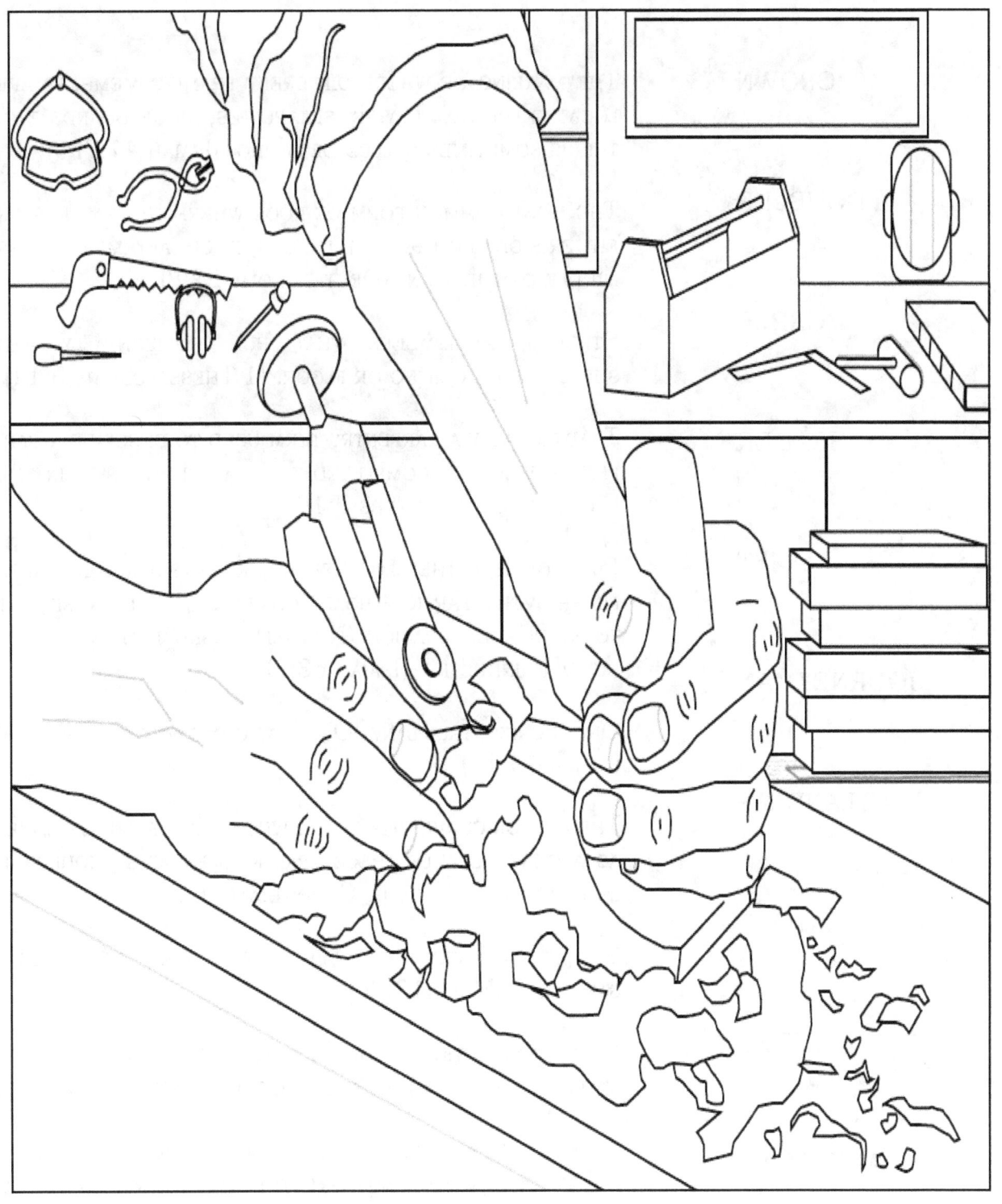

THE CARPENTER

MATCH THESE WORDS TO THEIR DEFINITIONS

CROWN

DOUBLER

GABLE

HEADER

JOIST

JOURNEYMAN

LANDING

LAYOUT

LEVEL

MELAMINE

THE MARKING OF WHERE DIFFERENT FRAMING MEMBERS ARE LOCATED ON WALL PLATES, SILL PLATES, RIDGE BOARDS ETC. THIS IS SOMETIMES CALLED DETAILING. (ISAIAH 41:7)

THE MOST COMMON FORM OF ROOF WHERE THE RAFTERS ON EITHER SIDE ARE THE SAME LENGTH, PITCH, AND MEET IN THE MIDDLE OF THE SPAN. (DEUTERONOMY 22:8)

STRUCTURAL MEMBERS THAT RUN HORIZONTALLY AND SUPPORTS THE CEILING OR FLOOR. (1 THESSALONIANS 5:14)

TRADITIONALLY A CARPENTRY TERM USED TO DESCRIBE A CARPENTER WHO HAS COMPLETED THEIR APPRENTICESHIP IN THE LOCAL UNION. (PROVERBS 7:19)

PLYWOOD IS A THERMALLY FUSED, RESIN SATURATED PAPER FINISH OVER A PARTICLE BOARD CORE. IT IS HIGHLY RESISTANT TO STAIN AND ABRASION. NORMALLY USED IN THE CABINET BUILDING INDUSTRY. (ISAIAH 63:3)

ON A HORIZONTAL PLANE. OR A BASIC CARPENTRY TOOL. (ISAIAH 44:13)

THE BOW OR CURVE OF A BOARD WHEN IT IS VIEWED ON EDGE, AS A GENERAL RULE THESE FRAMING MEMBERS SHOULD BE INSTALLED FACING UP. (1 CORINTHIANS 9:25)

STRUCTURAL MEMBERS NAILED TOGETHER FOR ADDED STRENGTH. (MARK 12:30)

IN CARPENTRY TERMS PLATFORM BETWEEN TWO FLIGHTS OF STAIRS TO ALLOW FOR A CHANGE OF DIRECTION. (JOHN 1:51)

A BEAM RUNNING HORIZONTALLY ABOVE WINDOW, DOOR, OR OTHER OPENING TO SUPPORT THE STRUCTURAL MEMBERS ABOVE IT. (MATTHEW 7:3-5)

DEFINITIONS: ANSWERS FOUND ON PAGE 36

SEE HOW MANY WORDS
YOU CAN BUILD OUT OF

KINDNESS

"FOR HIS MERCIFUL KINDNESS IS GREAT TOWARD US: AND THE TRUTH OF THE LORD ENDURETH FOR EVER. PRAISE YE THE LORD." ~ PSALM 117:2

_____

_____

_____

_____ _____

_____ _____

_____ _____

_____ _____

ABC'S OF CHARACTER
Find these words in the forest of letters

```
W N O B L E H F K W O R K E R P U O L O V I N G G
W I L T R S C C H I O E Q X D P B Z T Q U X I Z C
I N S I G U P U P V N U E V P D B N W O V M Z H I
F J S E Q U I T Y R E D Q W O Q U A L I T Y S O O
K K U O B A A Z R V T A N R L L H E R E S P E C T
L N R S S A C R I F I C E E P W U Z Y O C A M X B
R S G Z T C V A V F G F S M S U R N L U G E G P H
I N D U S T R I O U S E U R A S A E T F S E D A V
F P D U P K Y G R A C I O U S N E S S E Y M E T T
B R D Z I T C K Y Y O Q T F U J N F S N E X D I B
D C Z Y I E L D I N G M Q T Y K L E O V A R I E R
T F B L M H O N E S T Y P F U E B O R F Z X C N A
F O I T R U S T I N E S S S B X B B E S M Y A C V
T B O X B G J C R S R C O M P A S S I O N C T E E
A S S U N I T Y Q O N E N E S S V B X C W Y E K R
Q O L O T A U S T N B C W G G B U Z D X G L D Q Y
T N R F O R G I V E N E S S X K T V E X H U G W P
```

ABILITY	BRAVERY	COMPASSION	DEDICATED
EQUITY	FORGIVENESS	GRACIOUSNESS	HONESTY
INDUSTRIOUS	JUST	KINDNESS	LOVING
MANNERS	NOBLE	ONENESS	PATIENCE
QUALITY	RESPECT	SACRIFICE	TRUSTINESS
UNITY	VOLUNTEER	WORKER	YIELDING

Word Search 1: Answers found on page 35

10

SEE HOW MANY WORDS
YOU CAN BUILD OUT OF
OBEDIENCE

"So built we the wall; and all the wall was joined together unto the half thereof: for the people had a mind to work." ~ Nehemiah 4:6

_____

_____

_____

_____   _____

_____   _____

_____   _____

_____   _____

SECRET MESSAGE 2

A	B	C	D	E	F	G	H	I	J	K	L	M	N	O	P	Q	R	S	T	U	V	W	X	Y	Z
24	8	16	1	15	26	10	3	17	4	13	23	14	7	18	22	6	19	12	25	11	20	2	9	21	5

USE THE ABOVE KEYS TO DECODE THE MESSAGE BELOW

T H E   F L A K E S   O F
25 3 15   26 23 24 13 15 12   18 26

H I S   F L E S H   A R E
3 17 12   26 23 15 12 3   24 19 15

J O I N E D   T O G E T H E R :
4 18 17 7 15 1   25 18 10 15 25 3 15 19

T H E Y   A R E   F I R M
25 3 15 21   24 19 15   26 17 19 14

I N   T H E M S E L V E S ;
17 7   25 3 15 14 12 15 23 20 15 12

T H E Y   C A N N O T   B E
25 3 15 21   16 24 7 7 18 25   8 15

M O V E D .
14 18 20 15 1

WHERE IS THIS TEXT FOUND? _____

SECRET MESSAGE 2: ANSWERS FOUND ON PAGE 37

ABC'S OF CHARACTER
CROSSWORD PUZZLE 2

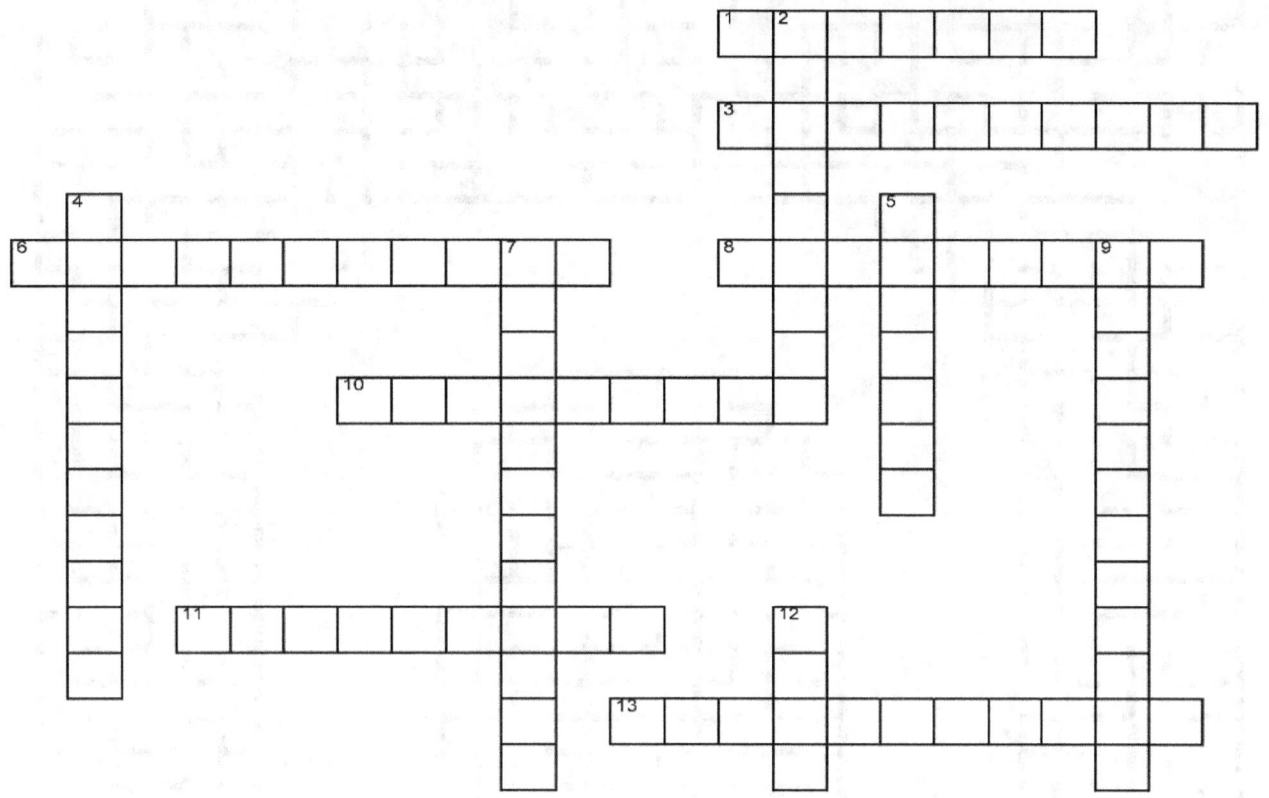

ACROSS

1. A FEELING OR ATTITUDE OF DEVOTED ATTACHMENT AND AFFECTION. FIDELITY TO A PRINCE OR SOVEREIGN.

3. CONSIDERATE OR KINDLY IN DISPOSITION; AMIABLE AND TENDER. TENDERNESS; SOFTNESS OF MANNERS.

6. THE ACT OR PRACTICE OF RECEIVING AND ENTERTAINING STRANGERS OR GUESTS WITHOUT REWARD.

8. SUBMISSION OR COURTEOUS YIELDING TO THE OPINION, WISHES, OR JUDGMENT OF ANOTHER. REGARD.

10. AN EMOTION OF THE HEART, EXCITED BY A FAVOR OR BENEFIT RECEIVED; THANKFULNESS.

11. EARNEST AND PERSISTENT APPLICATION TO AN UNDERTAKING; STEADY EFFORT.

13. REGULARITY; A STATE OF BEING METHODICAL.

DOWN

2. THE PERFORMANCE OF WHAT IS REQUIRED OR ENJOINED BY AUTHORITY, OR THE ABSTAINING FROM WHAT IS PROHIBITED, IN COMPLIANCE WITH THE COMMAND OR PROHIBITION.

4. A RESTING OR SATISFACTION OF MIND WITHOUT DISQUIET. A SOURCE OF SATISFACTION.

5. LABOR OF BODY OR OF BODY AND MIND, PERFORMED AT THE COMMAND OF A SUPERIOR, OR THE PURSUANCE OF DUTY, OR FOR THE BENEFIT OF ANOTHER.

7. FULL OF TRUTH.

9. BEING IN GOOD SPIRITS; REFLECTING WILLINGNESS OR GOOD HUMOR.

12. SHOWING PATIENCE AND HUMILITY; GENTLE. NOT PROUD OR SELF-SUFFICIENT.

CROSSWORD PUZZLE 2: ANSWERS FOUND ON PAGE 34

"NAVIGATION IS KEY IN THE WORD OF GOD"
SEEK AND FIND YOUR WAY THROUGH THE MAZE BELOW

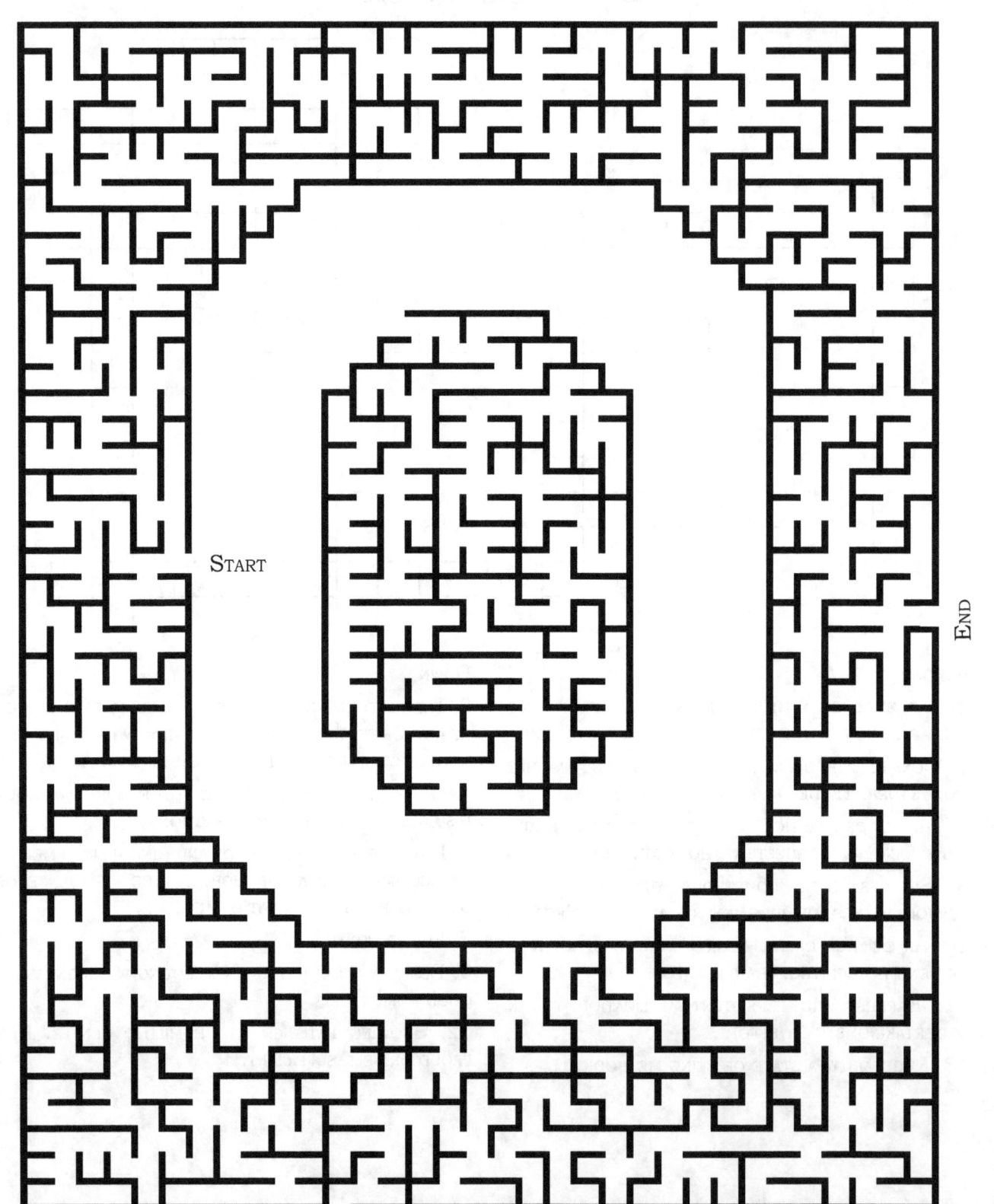

UNSCRAMBLE THESE WORDS THAT BUILD CHARACTER

ALYOLTY

_____

UUNROSISTID

_____

NAGCRI

_____

VECBLOEENEN

_____

IIVRGFONG

_____

SPTLEONIES

_____

RKOWRE

_____

SCMONSOIPA

_____

THAFLIUF

_____

YBVRERA

_____

UNSCRAMBLE EXERCISE: ANSWERS FOUND ON PAGE 37

WONDERFUL WORDS OF LIFE
FIND THESE WORDS IN THE FOREST OF LETTERS

```
Q F N M F Z F Z V L N B X U M Y A C K S Y B S K Y
L O E A V U I R I Y X W K G S B H W O E O V G T A
F C D V E O V E L A T T K F Z O X E C Y H S I M L
S O W T M R R N Q W I Z S F S C E N G M M L R H O
K N Y T R U T H F U L N E S S B E S L Q A X I N Y
A T D S X Q V Q H D U S E O B I J F B T L N R G A
Q E V Y B S D V N S N L H D O E I I Q U S O J L
U N O T L C H U E E I L D E G C K P R N N W Y C T
G T K M V J K C N L X Y B G N E S Q E F I S T O Y
T M O H R V I L R F D O C E B O N N S U C X Z T T
K E H F Y V U E D S E R R J H G E T P I F A G T T
A N W X R F D O K L W E Y F C Q F J L Z B P M A N
R T T E R R Z L I E F J Z W K V L Z Z E H W X Q O
B C S E O D L T E E W D I L I G E N C E N J J W P
Y I E L R S E N D L Z S K E G D A D Z S I E Z U H
I H G R A T I T U D E P G W P Y C O W Q J A S K T
C I Y M E E K W F O R L E W N L T V X A F R T S J
```

OBEDIENCE	ORDERLINESS	DILIGENCE	LOYALTY
DEFERENCE	GENTLENESS	MEEK	CONTENTMENT
GRATITUDE	TRUTHFULNESS	HOSPITALITY	SERVICE
CHEERFULNESS			

WORD SEARCH 2: ANSWERS FOUND ON PAGE 35

SECRET MESSAGE 3

A	B	C	D	E	F	G	H	I	J	K	L	M	N	O	P	Q	R	S	T	U	V	W	X	Y	Z
17	6	20	2	21	24	13	4	14	8	22	1	26	7	18	25	9	3	15	23	5	16	10	19	11	12

USE THE ABOVE KEYS TO DECODE THE MESSAGE BELOW

__   __ __ __ __   __ __ __   __ __ __ __ __ ,
14   22 7 18 10   23 4 11   10 18 3 22 15

__ __ __   __ __ __ __ __ __ __ ,   __ __ __
17 7 2   20 4 17 3 14 23 11   17 7 2

__ __ __ __ __ __ __ ,   __ __ __
15 21 3 16 14 20 21   17 7 2

__ __ __ __ __ ,   __ __ __   __ __ __
24 17 14 23 4   17 7 2   23 4 11

__ __ __ __ __ __ __ __ ,   __ __ __
25 17 23 14 21 7 20 21   17 7 2

__ __ __   __ __ __ __ __ ;   __ __ __
23 4 11   10 18 3 22 15   17 7 2

__ __ __   __ __ __ __   __ __
23 4 21   1 17 15 23   23 18

__ __   __ __ __ __   __ __ __ __
6 21   26 18 3 21   23 4 17 7

__ __ __   __ __ __ __ __ .
23 4 21   24 14 3 15 23

WHERE IS THIS TEXT FOUND: _____

SECRET MESSAGE 3: ANSWERS FOUND ON PAGE 37

BUILDING BLOCKS OF CHARACTER
CROSSWORD PUZZLE 3

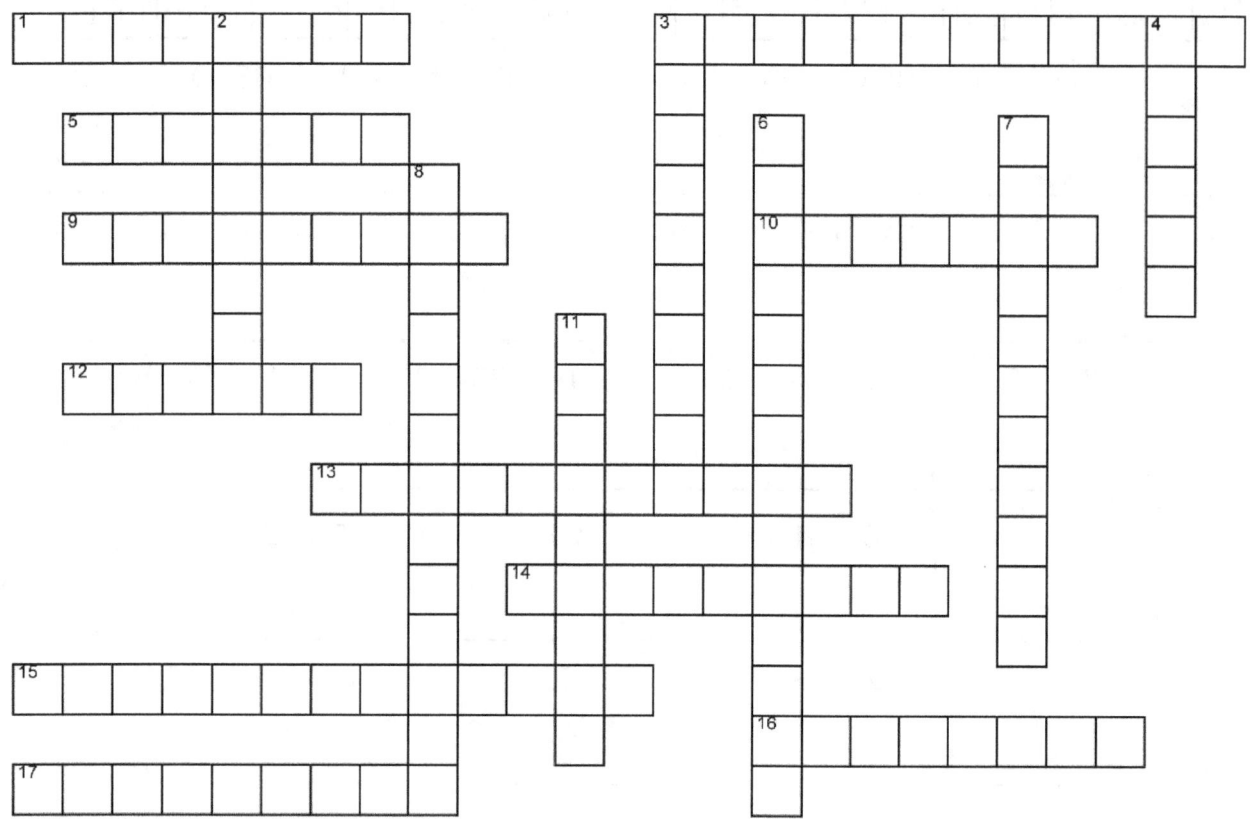

ACROSS

1. THE STATE OF BEING ACCOUNTABLE OR ANSWERABLE, AS FOR A TRUST OR OFFICE, OR FOR A DEBT.

3. PERSISTENCE IN ANY THING UNDERTAKEN; APPLIED ALIKE TO GOOD OR EVIL.

5. TO EXERCISE AUTHORITATIVE OR DOMINATING INFLUENCE OVER. POWER; AUTHORITY; COMMAND.

9. TO MAKE AN EFFORT TO HEAR SOMETHING.

10. PARTAKING; HAVING A PART WITH ANOTHER; ENJOYING OR SUFFERING WITH OTHERS.

12. A PERSON WHOM ONE KNOWS, LIKES, AND TRUSTS.

13. THE STATE OF BEING VESTED WITH THE RIGHTS AND PRIVILEGES OF A CITIZEN.

14. A BASIC TRUTH, LAW, OR ASSUMPTION.

15. RECEIVING FAVORABLE; AGREEING TO; UNDERSTANDING.

16. COOPERATIVE EFFORT BY THE MEMBERS OF A GROUP TO ACHIEVE A COMMON GOAL.

17. RECEIVING SOMETHING OFFERED, ESPECIALLY WITH GLADNESS OR APPROVAL.

DOWN

2. A POSITION OF THE BODY OR MANNER OF CARRYING ONESELF. POSTURE; POSITION OF THINGS OR PERSONS.

3. MARKED BY OR SHOWING CONSIDERATION FOR OTHERS, TACT, AND OBSERVANCE OF ACCEPTED SOCIAL USAGE.

4. FEELING AND EXHIBITING CONCERN AND EMPATHY FOR OTHERS.

6. THE STATE OF BEING ACCOUNTABLE OR ANSWERABLE, AS FOR A TRUST OR OFFICE, OR FOR A DEBT.

7. ACTING OR ARRIVING EXACTLY AT THE TIME APPOINTED; PROMPT.

8. A DISPOSITION TO APPRECIATE OR SHARE THE FEELINGS AND THOUGHTS OF OTHERS; SYMPATHY.

11. STEADFAST ADHERENCE TO A STRICT MORAL OR ETHICAL CODE. WHOLENESS; ENTIRENESS; UNBROKEN STATE.

CROSSWORD PUZZLE 3: ANSWERS FOUND ON PAGE 34

FILL IN THE BLANK
COMMIT THESE VERSES OF SCRIPTURE TO MEMORY

AND THERE WAS ONE _____, A _____, THE _____ OF _____, OF THE TRIBE OF _____: SHE WAS OF A _____ AGE, AND HAD _____ WITH AN HUSBAND _____ YEARS FROM HER _____. ~ LUKE 2:36

AND SHE CAME IN _____ WITH _____ UNTO THE _____, AND ASKED, SAYING, I WILL THAT THOU _____ ME BY AND BY IN A _____ THE HEAD OF _____ THE _____. ~ MARK 6:25

I ____ THAT _____ OF _____. ~ JOHN 6:48

AND WHEN THEY WERE _____, BEHOLD, THE _____ OF THE LORD _____ TO _____ IN A _____, SAYING, ARISE, AND _____ THE YOUNG _____ AND HIS _____, AND FLEE INTO _____, AND BE _____ THERE UNTIL I _____ THEE _____: FOR _____ WILL _____ THE _____ CHILD TO _____ HIM. ~ MATTHEW 2:13

FROM _____ YEARS OLD AND _____ EVEN UNTO _____ YEARS OLD, _____ ONE THAT _____ INTO THE _____, FOR THE _____ IN THE _____ OF THE _____. ~ NUMBERS 4:39

AND _____ HE WAS OF THE SAME _____, HE _____ WITH THEM, AND _____: FOR BY THEIR _____ THEY WERE _____. ~ ACTS 18:3

THEN _____ HE TO THE _____, BEHOLD THY _____! AND FROM THAT _____ THAT _____ TOOK HER UNTO HIS OWN _____. ~ JOHN 19:27

AND _____ WAS _____ WITH _____ HAIR, AND WITH A _____ OF A _____ ABOUT HIS _____; AND HE DID EAT _____ AND WILD _____. ~ MARK 1:6

AND SHE _____ OUT WITH A _____ VOICE, AND _____, BLESSED ART THOU _____ _____, AND _____ IS THE _____ OF THY _____. ~ LUKE 1:42

SEE HOW MANY WORDS
YOU CAN BUILD OUT OF
MEEKNESS

"WHAT WILL YE? SHALL I COME UNTO YOU WITH A ROD, OR IN LOVE, AND IN THE SPIRIT OF MEEKNESS?"
~ 1 CORINTHIANS 4:21

_____

_____

_____

_____   _____

_____   _____

_____   _____

_____   _____

BUILDING BLOCKS OF CHARACTER

FIND THESE WORDS IN THE FOREST OF LETTERS

```
N P Q T G G N Q U U P V T G U S J G R B S I U Y Q
L I C M W I I Z V F D L I P O L I T E N E S S B M
E J B C D L C A N D E U J A C C E P T I N G O V B
C R X O L I U O P P P D U N D E R S T A N D I N G
B M T N Q S M Y R L E P C C N L A K I Z M L F G S
S E K T C T J B I M N R C X C R B T V N L R F R H
M H E R D E K Y Z U D P S I P R A U T Y N J R G A
C M K O O N R E L I A N C E T R I C J I E X I K R
B T G L Z I E K W U B I E I V I I W A F T W E T I
C E Y Q A N T A P M I T N V K E Z N V R Z U N Y N
K A F W R G A A Y H L L E T H B R E C B I U D C G
K M A I L R V H A E I N I Q E J G A N I I N V E P
C W W D Q R F X E I T I M G N G Z X N S P S G H B
H O Q N C E D P J M Y M L A M C R W R C H L I A C
R R F Z E Q R E S P O N S I B I L I T Y E I E U J
A K E G M H S V F P R K G Q R U K Z T T G O P W L
P U N C T U A L I T Y B K M Y B M M U Y K L B T E
```

ATTITUDE	ACCEPTING	CARING	CITIZENSHIP
CONTROL	DEPENDABILITY	FRIEND	INTEGRITY
LISTENING	POLITENESS	PUNCTUALITY	PRINCIPLE
RELIANCE	TEAMWORK	UNDERSTANDING	RESPONSIBILITY
SHARING	PERSEVERANCE		

WORD SEARCH 3: ANSWERS FOUND ON PAGE 35

SEE HOW MANY WORDS
YOU CAN BUILD OUT OF

GENTLENESS

"BUT THE FRUIT OF THE SPIRIT IS LOVE, JOY, PEACE, LONGSUFFERING, GENTLENESS, GOODNESS, FAITH." ~ GALATIANS 5:22

OBJECTIVES OF CHARACTER
CROSSWORD PUZZLE 4

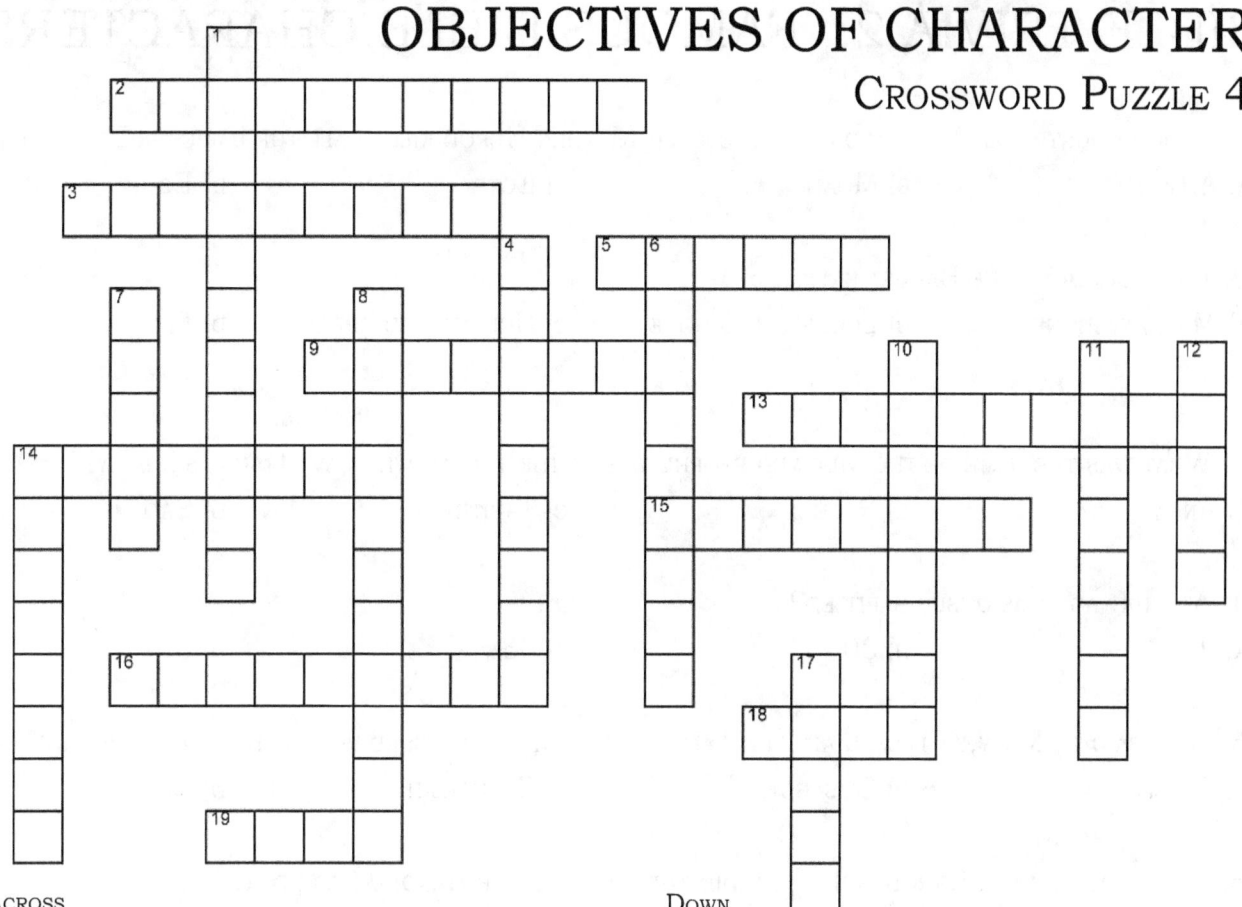

ACROSS

2. FREEDOM FROM DIRT, FILTH, OR ANY FOUL, EXTRANEOUS MATTER. NEATNESS OF PERSON OR DRESS; PURITY.

3. THE CAPACITY TO ENDURE HARDSHIP OR PAIN.

5. HONORABLE; ADMIRABLE. SUITABLE; HAVING QUALITIES SUITED TO; EQUAL IN VALUE; AS FLOWERS WORTHY OF PARADISE.

9. KINDNESS; BENEVOLENCE OF NATURE; MERCY. GENEROSITY; KINDNESS. MORAL EXCELLENCE; PIETY; VIRTUE.

13. BEARING; ENDURING; UPHOLDING; SUSTAINING; MAINTAINING; SUBSISTING; VINDICATING.

14. OF PLEASING APPEARANCE, ESPECIALLY BECAUSE OF A PURE OR FRESH QUALITY; COMELY. OPENNESS, CANDOR.

15. ADHERENCE TO THE TRUTH; TRUTHFULNESS. CONFORMITY TO FACT OR TRUTH; ACCURACY OR PRECISION. HABITUAL TRUTH.

16. EXERCISING MODERATION AND SELF-RESTRAINT. THE POWER OR CAPACITY OF ENDURING.

18. A DEEP, TENDER, INEFFABLE FEELING OF AFFECTION AND SOLICITUDE TOWARD A PERSON. BENEVOLENCE; GOOD WILL.

19. PLEASING AND AGREEABLE IN NATURE. TENDER; DAINTY; DELICATE.

DOWN

1. THE LOVE OF MANKIND ACCOMPANIED WITH A DESIRE TO PROMOTE THEIR HAPPINESS.

4. RESPECTED; WORTHY OF RESPECT; REGARDED WITH ESTEEM. DISTINGUISHED; ILLUSTRIOUS.

6. TAKING NOTICE; ATTENTIVELY VIEWING OR NOTICING; AS AN OBSERVANT SPECTATOR OR TRAVELER.

7. A QUALITY DESERVING PRAISE OR APPROVAL; VIRTUE. VALUE; EXCELLENCE.

8. HAVING OR MARKED BY REGARD FOR THE NEEDS OR FEELINGS OF OTHERS.

10. AN INHERENT ABILITY, AS FOR LEARNING; A TALENT. FITNESS; SUITABLENESS. READINESS IN LEARNING.

11. SEPARATE OR DISTINCT IN FORM OR CONCEPT. CONSISTING OF UNCONNECTED DISTINCT PARTS.

12. A STATE OF QUIET OR TRANQUILITY; FREEDOM FROM DISTURBANCE OR AGITATION. FREEDOM FROM QUARRELS AND DISAGREEMENT; HARMONIOUS RELATIONS.

14. ADHERING FIRMLY AND DEVOTEDLY, AS TO A PERSON, CAUSE, OR IDEA; LOYAL.

17. CONFORMING TO STANDARDS OF WHAT IS RIGHT OR JUST IN BEHAVIOR; VIRTUOUS.

CROSSWORD PUZZLE 4: ANSWERS FOUND ON PAGE 34

BIBLE TRIVIA 2: FAMOUS BIBLE CHARACTERS

1. WHICH COUNTRY DID MARY AND JOSEPH ESCAPE TO WHEN HEROD KILLED ALL THE BABIES IN BETHLEHEM?

A) AMMON   B) MOAB   C) EGYPT   D) EDOM

2. WHAT DID JOHN THE BAPTIST EAT?

A) MILK AND HONEY   B) LOCUSTS AND HONEY   C) UNLEAVENED BREAD   D) FIGS AND POMEGRANATES

3. WHAT WAS THE NAME OF THE WIDOWED PROPHETESS AT THE TEMPLE WHO SAW JESUS AS A BABY?

A) ANNA   B) RACHEL   C) TABITHA   D) SALOME

4. AT WHAT AGE WAS JESUS BAPTIZED?

A) 25   B) 30   C) 33   D) 35

5. WHO SAID TO MARY, "BLESSED ART THOU AMONG WOMEN, AND BLESSED IS THE FRUIT OF THY WOMB!"?

A) JOSEPH   B) ELISABETH   C) ZECHARIAH   D) SIMEON

6. AFTER DANCING FOR HEROD, WHAT GIFT DID THE DAUGHTER OF HERODIAS ASK FOR?

A) HALF THE KINGDOM   B) JOHN THE BAPTIST'S DEAD BODY   C) JOHN THE BAPTIST'S HEAD   D) MONEY

7. WHAT WAS PAUL'S PROFESSION?

A) TENTMAKER   B) CARPENTER   C) TAX COLLECTOR   D) FISHERMAN

8. WHICH DISCIPLE TOOK CARE OF MARY AFTER THE DEATH OF JESUS?

A) JAMES   B) PETER   C) SIMON   D) JOHN

9. WHAT DOES THE NAME "MATTHEW" MEAN?

A) THE LORD IS HERE   B) GIFT OF THE LORD   C) TREASURES OF THE LORD   D) THE LORD IS MERCIFUL

10. IN WHICH GOSPEL DOES JESUS SAY THAT HE IS THE "BREAD OF LIFE"?

A) MATTHEW   B) MARK   C) LUKE   D) JOHN

BIBLE TRIVIA 2: ANSWERS FOUND ON PAGE 36

"NAVIGATION IS KEY IN THE WORD OF GOD"

SEEK AND FIND YOUR WAY THROUGH THE MAZE BELOW

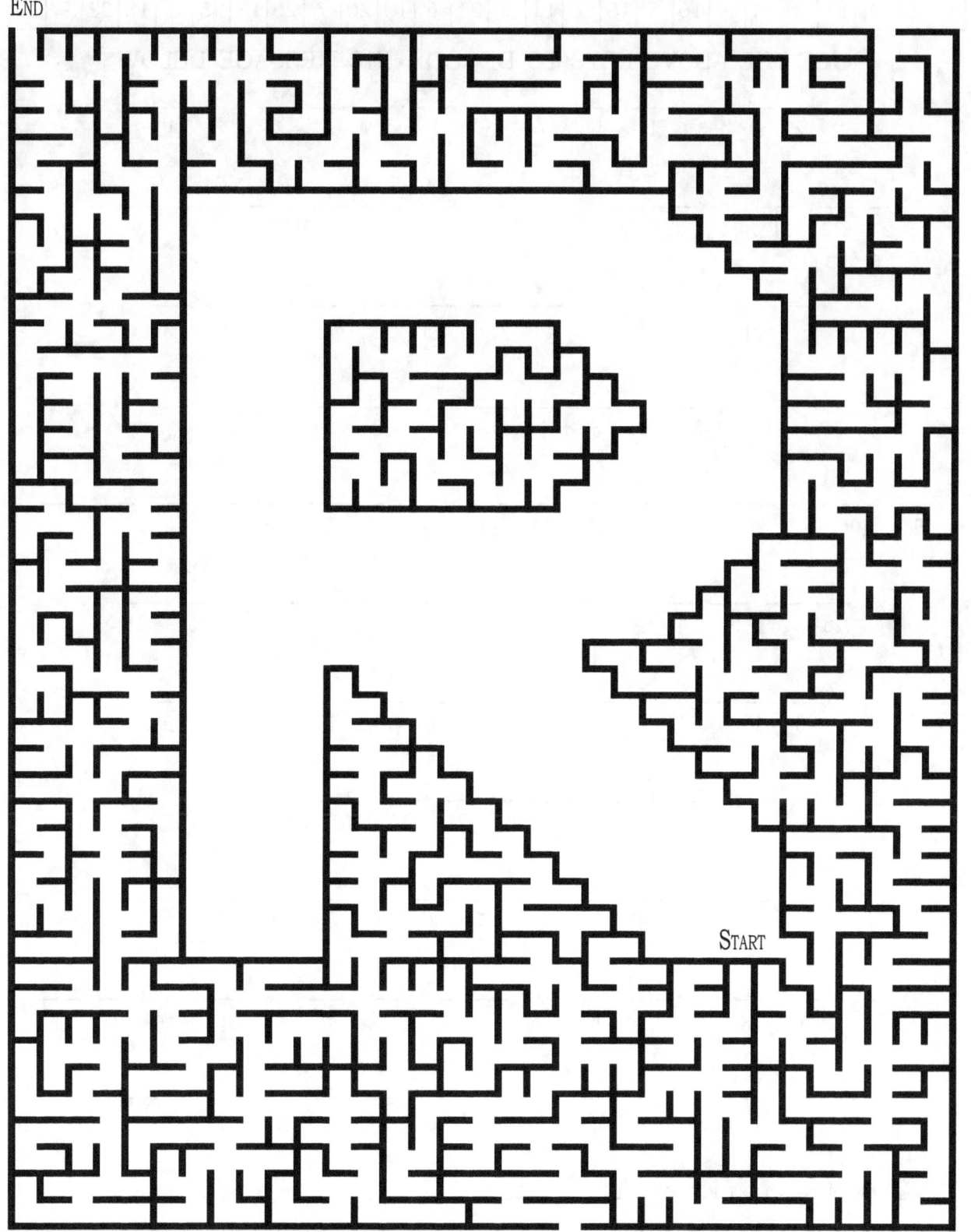

SECRET MESSAGE 3

A	B	C	D	E	F	G	H	I	J	K	L	M	N	O	P	Q	R	S	T	U	V	W	X	Y	Z
12	22	4	17	3	14	24	16	5	18	1	11	2	21	6	10	20	7	26	13	25	8	15	23	9	19

USE THE ABOVE KEYS TO DECODE THE MESSAGE BELOW

BRETHREN, IF A

MAN BE OVERTAKEN

IN A FAULT, YE

WHICH ARE

SPIRITUAL, RESTORE

SUCH AN ONE IN

THE SPIRIT OF

MEEKNESS;

CONSIDERING

THYSELF, LEST THOU

ALSO BE TEMPTED.

WHERE IS THIS TEXT FOUND: _____

SECRET MESSAGE 4: ANSWERS FOUND ON PAGE 37

FILL IN THE BLANK
COMMIT THESE VERSES OF SCRIPTURE TO MEMORY

AND _____ STOOD, AND SAID UNTO THE _____; BEHOLD, LORD, THE _____ OF MY _____ I _____ TO THE _____; AND IF I HAVE _____ ANY _____ FROM ANY MAN BY _____ _____, I _____ HIM _____. ~ LUKE 19:8

AND _____ AND _____, THE SONS OF _____, COME UNTO _____, SAYING, _____, WE _____ THAT THOU _____ DO FOR US _____ WE SHALL _____. ~ MARK 10:35

_____ ARE THE _____: FOR _____ SHALL _____ THE _____. ~ MATTHEW 5:5

AND THEY CAME TO _____: AND AS HE _____ OUT OF _____ WITH HIS _____ AND A _____ NUMBER OF _____, _____ BARTIMAEUS , THE SON OF _____, _____ BY THE _____ SIDE _____. ~ MARK 10:46

AND, _____, THERE _____ A MAN NAMED _____, AND _____ WAS A _____ OF THE SYNAGOGUE: AND HE _____ DOWN AT _____ FEET, AND _____ HIM THAT HE _____ COME INTO HIS _____. ~ LUKE 8:41

AND _____ UNTO THEM, WHAT _____ YE _____ ME, AND I WILL _____ HIM _____ YOU? AND THEY _____ WITH HIM FOR _____ PIECES OF _____. ~ MATTHEW 26:15

THERE WAS A _____ OF THE _____, NAMED _____, A _____ OF THE _____. ~ JOHN 3:1

SO _____ CAME _____ INTO _____ OF _____, WHERE HE _____ THE _____ _____. AND THERE WAS A CERTAIN _____, WHOSE _____ WAS SICK AT _____. ~ JOHN 4:46

AND _____ HIM AWAY TO _____ FIRST; FOR HE WAS _____ IN _____ TO _____, WHICH WAS THE _____ _____ THAT SAME _____. ~ JOHN 18:13

NOW A _____ MAN WAS _____, NAMED _____, OF _____, THE TOWN OF _____ AND HER SISTER _____. ~ JOHN 11:1

27

OBJECTIVES OF CHARACTER

FIND THESE WORDS IN THE FOREST OF LETTERS

```
D H O A G A B Z Q Y L R Y S K E X P H K N I C E W
S T G Q J G V W Y B T C S N P A P T I T U D E E C
D E Z G Y L O V E Z I E T O C F L G W X B J V V S
P H B M A X P I U E N K I D N D A E R Y H I J S O
I P H M O S N S Z D K S L U C X T I B N T G E X B
B D S C W R V M O D D T N R C A T K T R G N Y U S
T P B M C S A O C S I S I O R I B E O H I B I E E
V K P E B K G L Y C S V Z E M C L P Q L F S Z A R
Q Z R R N E R T J E C M P L U B P U N J G U R V V
X T M I B E I T N Y R M Q R A U M A C B W J L W A
T M B T G C V R K E E M Y R S A E D L H B H R P N
H M S S A B I O F T T U O A E L V S A P N R V D T
E G R R W A M S L E E N N Y C J H X T V X V O O C
Q F E C F K H S H E O T H H G S X K B B S E J H Q
X V Y P E A C E D H N H R W C O N S I D E R A T E
W L Z P F L Q N Q D L C C D G G J E D M E T D A E
I K W O R T H Y O K U G E H B T O L E R A N C E E
```

APTITUDE	BENEVOLENCE	CONSIDERATE	CLEANLINESS	DISCRETE
FAIRNESS	FAITHFUL	GOODNESS	HONORABLE	LOVE
MERIT	MORAL	NICE	OBSERVANT	PEACE
SUPPORTIVE	TOLERANCE	TEMPERATE	WORTHY	VERACITY

WORD SEARCH 4: ANSWERS FOUND ON PAGE 35

MATCH THESE WORDS TO THEIR DEFINITIONS

RIDGE

ANY WALL WHICH DOES NOT SUPPORT ANY WEIGHT SUCH AS FLOOR FRAMING, ROOF FRAMING, OR CEILING JOISTS.

PLATE

IN ROOF FRAMING THE HIGHEST POINT OF THE COMMON RAFTERS.

NONBEARING WALL

BASICALLY THIS IS JUST A LARGE ROUGH TERRAIN FORKLIFT USED TO MOVE AND ACCESS MATERIAL AROUND MUCH MORE EFFICIENTLY ON THE JOB SITE. THIS MACHINE CAN EASILY BECOME YOUR BEST FRIEND. ESPECIALLY WHEN ROOF FRAMING.

RUN

THE TOP AND BOTTOM PLATE IN A WALL.

TRIMMER

ON A VERTICAL PLANE, OR UP AND DOWN, AS IN WHEN SOMEONE SAYS "LEVEL THAT WALL" THE CORRECT CARPENTRY TERM IS PLUMB THAT WALL.

STRINGER

THE VARIOUS FRAMING MEMBERS FOR THE ROOF OF A BUILDING.

PETTIBONE

THE PEAK OR UPPERMOST PORTION OF A SLOPED ROOF.

VALLEY

THE HORIZONTAL DISTANCE COVERED BY ONE STEP, SET OF STEPS, OR A SINGLE RAFTER, NORMALLY HALF THE WIDTH OF THE AREA COVERED BY THE ROOF.

RAFTER

THE MAIN SUPPORT FOR A STAIRCASE, WHICH THE RISERS AND TREADS ARE ATTACHED TO.

PEAK

THE FRAMING MEMBER NAILED TO THE KING STUD UNDER THE END OF THE HEADER TO SUPPORT THE WEIGHT FROM ABOVE.

PLUMB

WHERE TWO DIFFERENT ROOF SLOPES INTERSECT.

DEFINITIONS: ANSWERS FOUND ON PAGE 36

COLORING ACTIVITY

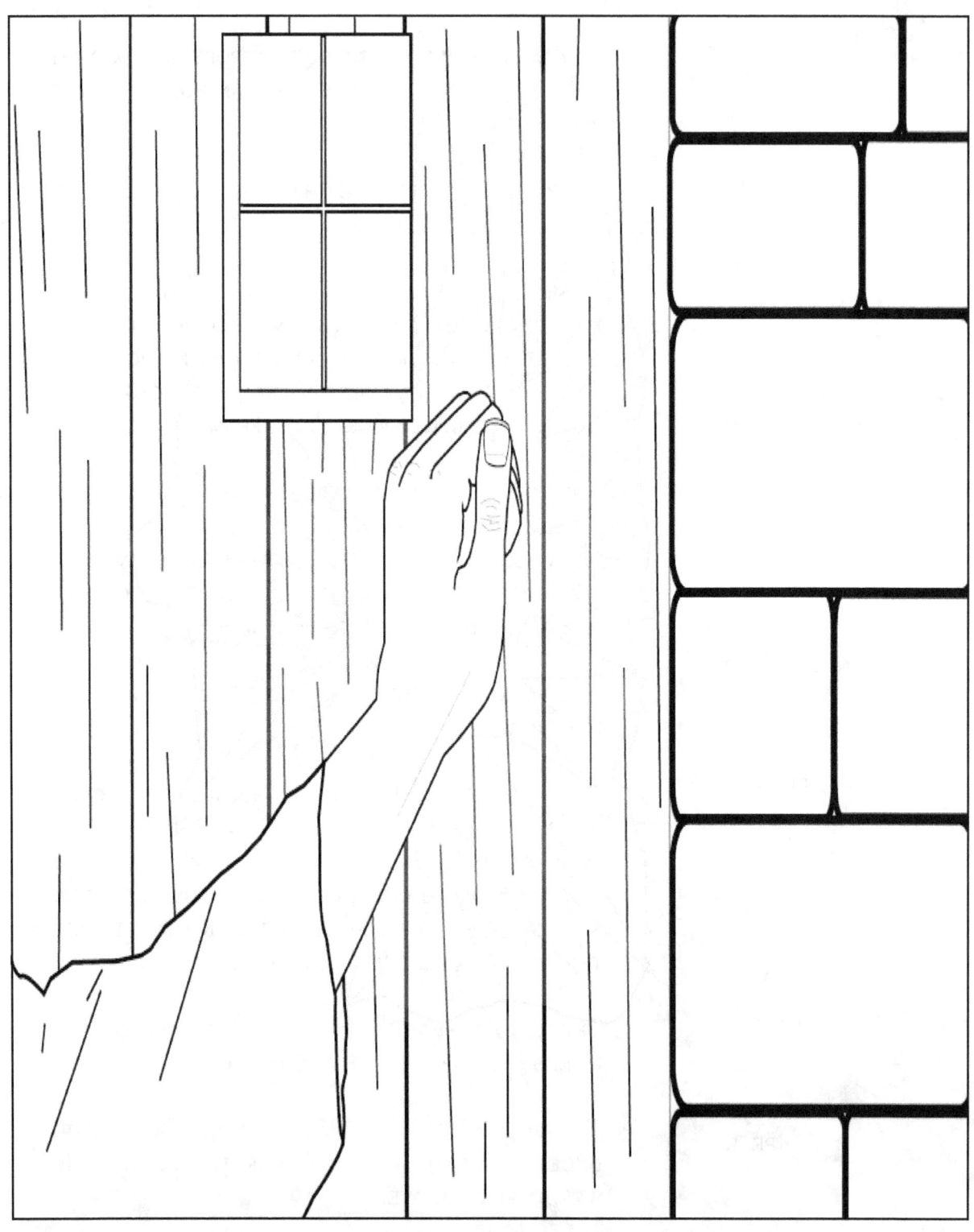

THE KNOCK

"NAVIGATION IS KEY IN THE WORD OF GOD"
SEEK AND FIND YOUR WAY THROUGH THE MAZE BELOW

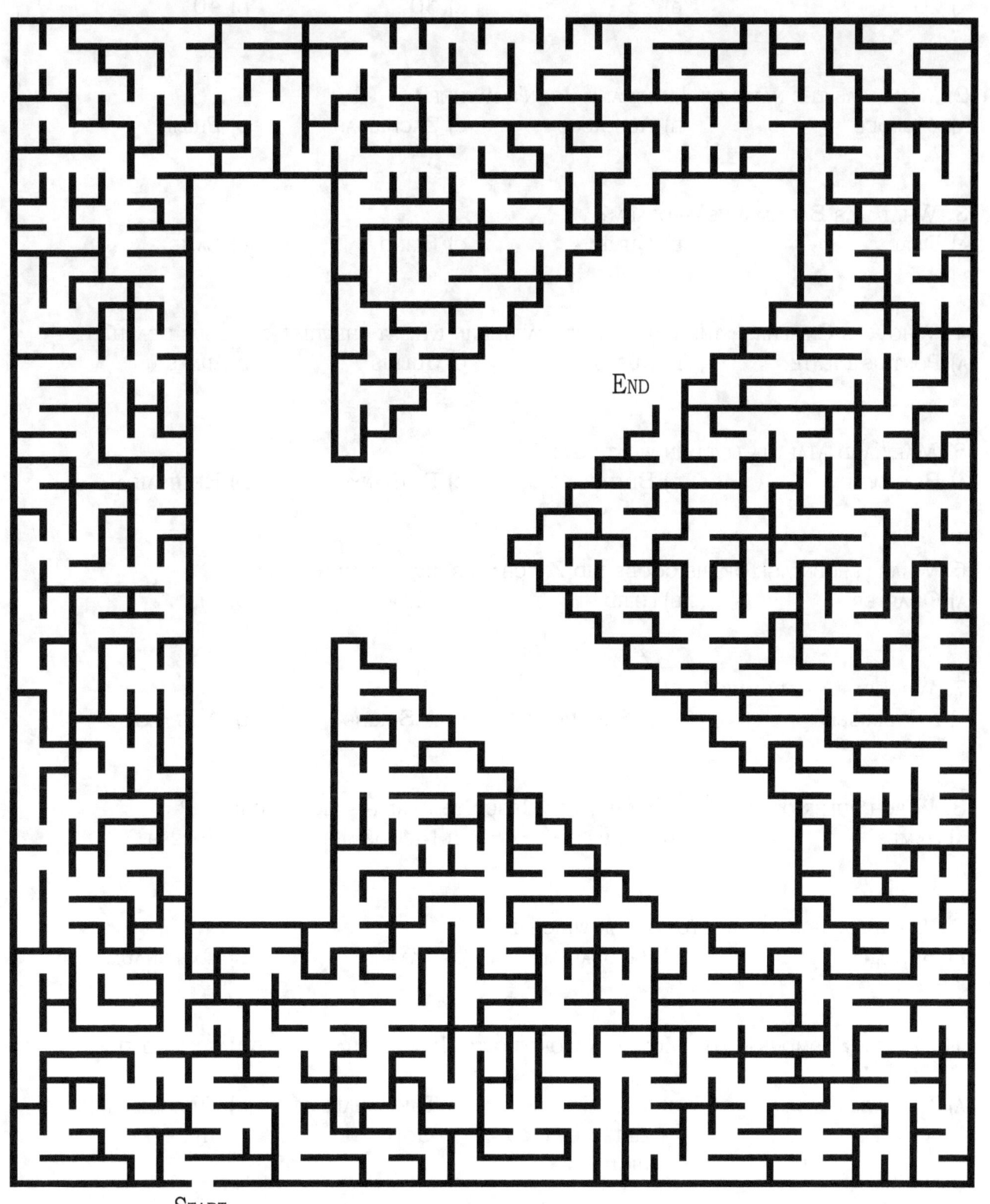

END

START

BIBLE TRIVIA 3: FAMOUS BIBLE CHARACTERS

1. Jesus was betrayed for how many pieces of silver by Judas Iscariot?
A) 20
B) 25
C) 30
D) 40

2. What was the name of James and John's father?
A) Zebedee
B) Alphaeus
C) Zacharias
D) Philip

3. What was Bartimaeus' problem?
A) Deaf
B) Dumb
C) Blind
D) Lame

4. Who was Caiaphas', the high priest, father in law at the time of Jesus death?
A) Pontius Pilate
B) Justus
C) Julius
D) Annas

5. Mary and Martha lived in what town?
A) Bethlehem
B) Bethel
C) Bethany
D) Bethsaida

6. What percentage of his goods did Zacchaeus give to the poor?
A) Quarter
B) Third
C) Half
D) All

7. Who was Nicodemus?
A) A Pharisee
B) A Sadducee
C) A Scribe
D) A Zealot

8. Which ruler of the synagogue asked Jesus to heal his sick daughter?
A) James
B) Jairus
C) Nicodemus
D) Joseph

9. Jesus turned water into wine in which town?
A) Bethany
B) Jerusalem
C) Cana
D) Capernaum

10. In the Sermon on the Mount, according to Jesus, what would happen to the meek?
A) They will obtain mercy
B) They will be lifted up on high
C) They shall see God
D) They will inherit the earth

Bible Trivia 3: Answers found on page 36

SEE HOW MANY WORDS
YOU CAN BUILD OUT OF

GOODNESS

"AND JETHRO REJOICED FOR ALL THE GOODNESS WHICH THE LORD HAD DONE TO ISRAEL, WHOM HE HAD DELIVERED OUT OF THE HAND OF THE EGYPTIANS." ~ EXODUS 18:9

_____

_____

_____

_____   _____

_____   _____

_____   _____

_____   _____

ANSWER PAGES

CROSSWORD 1

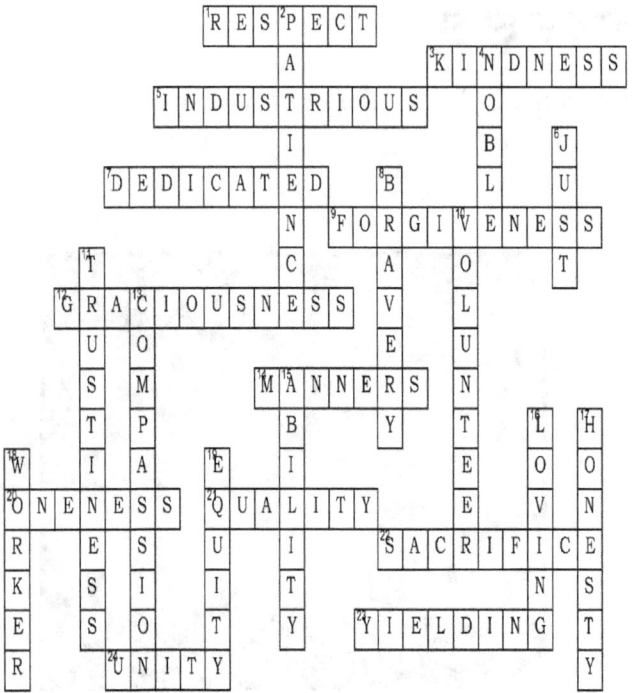

CROSSWORD 2

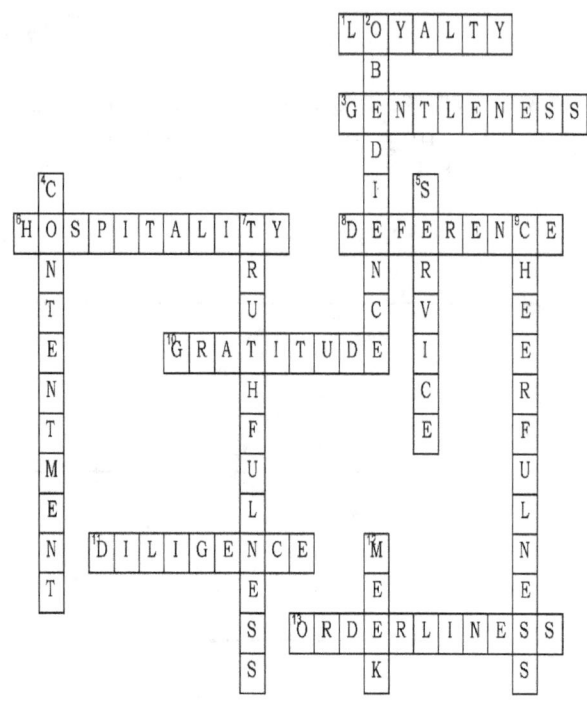

CROSSWORD 3

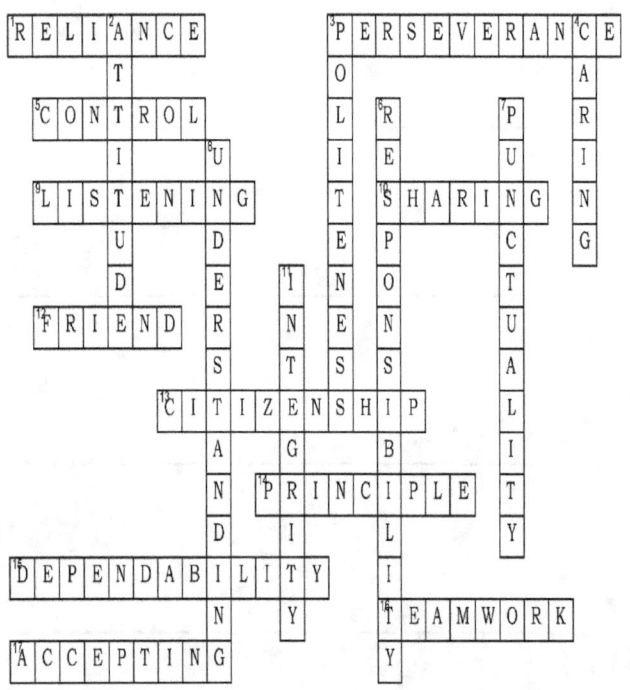

CROSSWORD 4

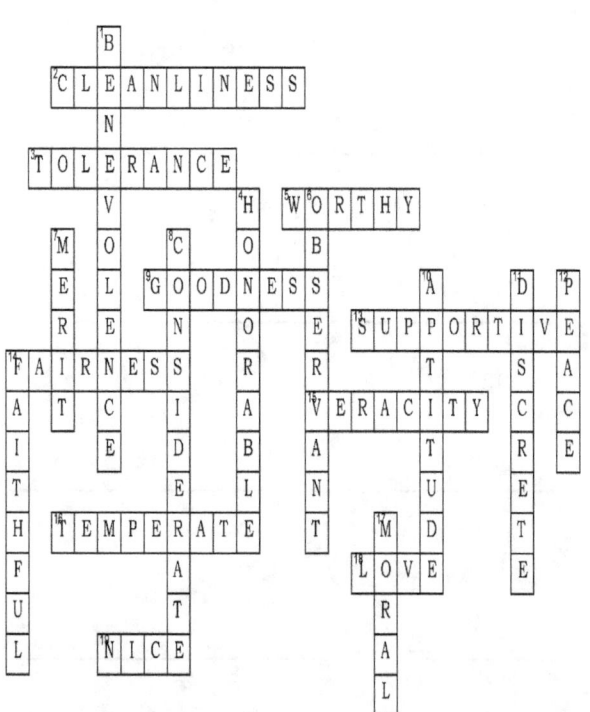

Word Search 1

```
W N O B L E H F K W O R K E R P U O L O V I N G G
W I L T R S C C H I O E Q X D P B Z T Q U X I Z C
I N S I G U P U P V N U E V P D B N W O V M Z H I
F J S E Q U I T Y R E D Q W O Q U A L I T Y S O O
K K U O B A A Z R V T A N R L L H E R E S P E C T
L N R S S A C R I F I C E E P W U Z Y O C A M X B
R S G Z T C V A V F G F S M S U R N L U G E G P H
I N D U S T R I O U S E U R A S A E T F S E D A V
F P D U P K Y G R A C I O U S N E S S E Y M E T T
B R D Z I T C K Y Y O Q T F U J N F S N E X D I B
D C Z Y I E L D I N G M Q T Y K L E O V A R I E R
T F B L M H O N E S T Y P F U E B O R F Z X C N A
F O I T R U S T I N E S S S B X B B E S M Y A C V
T B O X B G J C R S R C O M P A S S I O N C T E E
A S S U N I T Y Q O N E N E S S V B X C W Y E K R
Q O L O T A U S T N B C W G G B U Z D X G L D Q Y
T N R F O R G I V E N E S S X K T V E X H U G W P
```

Word Search 2

```
E O T P G F I R S T F R U I T S G N U Q B L A Y J
I Q P Z Y D B N W W J F D A V I D U W Z D H A X O
C V B O E V E R L A S T I N G F A T H E R A S N T
B R E A D O F L I F E S V F J L A K Z E I H B F S
Q F E V A B Y X H J L M W X J P M D B R S V I A Z
V O T H N B Y F L U N E H B F Z Y L X Y B N Y C K
M U E P H G G S F T I F O U N T A I N B P S N P U
A N R S C D U H D D M Y W C R M J Z J O T O M J Y
L D N R P M T G A E L E C T O F G O D I Y J P C F
M A A G R I H Q C H P U J F I R S T A N D L A S T
I T L S A C C D A Y S P R I N G Q V H T F D O O R
G I L F F O R E R U N N E R J O G E M M A N U E L
H O I G E T W Q N E Q Y D E E F R I E N D N U M I
T N F E D I A D E M I U A A X U O R J I U A Q G H
Y M E F I R S T B E G O T T E N V D A Y S T A R Z
B P F I R S T B O R N J M O S A V Z S S J S T D V
H F E X T Q E L K N V L E D E L I V E R E R P R Q
```

Word Search 3

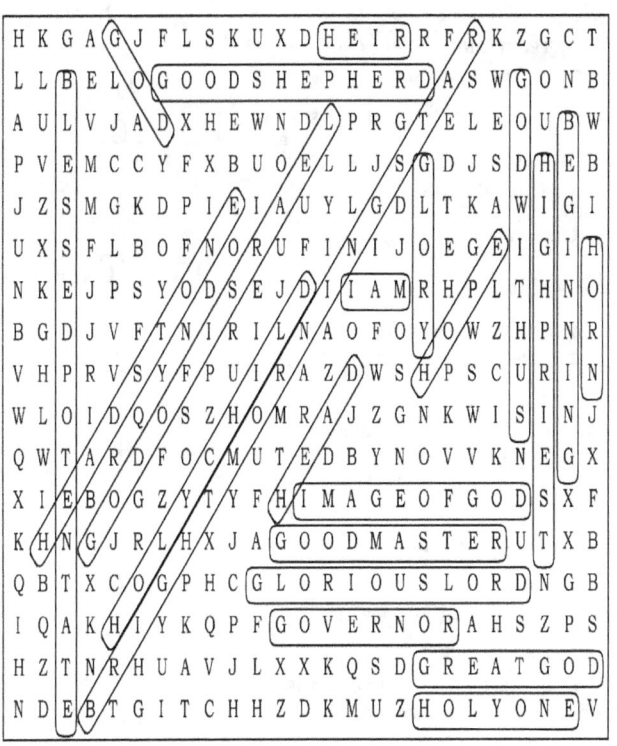

Word Search 4

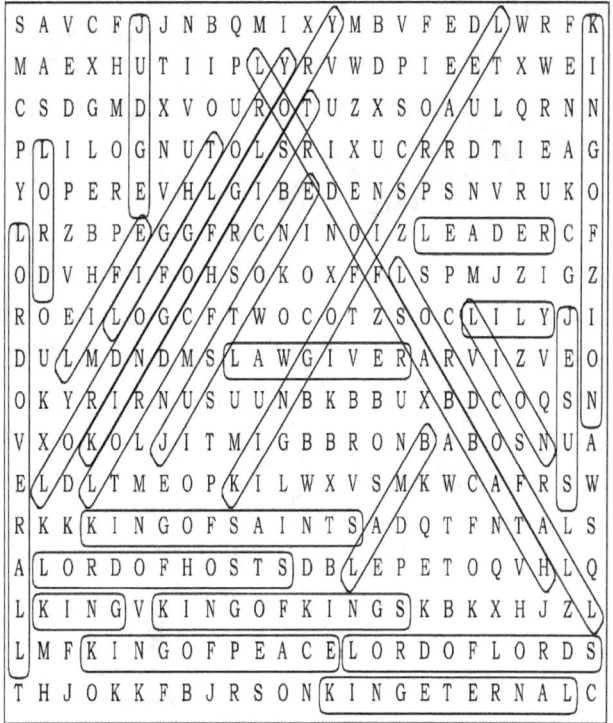

Definitions 1

CROWN

DOUBLER

GABLE

HEADER

JOIST

JOURNEYMAN

LANDING

LAYOUT

LEVEL

MELAMINE

THE MARKING OF WHERE DIFFERENT FRAMING MEMBERS ARE LOCATED ON WALL PLATES, SILL PLATES, RIDGE BOARDS ETC. THIS IS SOMETIMES CALLED DETAILING.

THE MOST COMMON FORM OF ROOF WHERE THE RAFTERS ON EITHER SIDE ARE THE SAME LENGTH, PITCH, AND MEET IN THE MIDDLE OF THE SPAN.

STRUCTURAL MEMBERS THAT RUN HORIZONTALLY AND SUPPORTS THE CEILING OR FLOOR.

TRADITIONALLY A CARPENTRY TERM USED TO DESCRIBE A CARPENTER WHO HAS COMPLETED THEIR APPRENTICESHIP IN THE LOCAL UNION.

PLYWOOD IS A THERMALLY FUSED, RESIN SATURATED PAPER FINISH OVER A PARTICLE BOARD CORE. IT IS HIGHLY RESISTANT TO STAIN AND ABRASION. NORMALLY USED IN THE CABINET BUILDING INDUSTRY.

ON A HORIZONTAL PLANE. OR A BASIC CARPENTRY TOOL.

THE BOW OR CURVE OF A BOARD WHEN IT IS VIEWED ON EDGE, AS A GENERAL RULE THESE FRAMING MEMBERS SHOULD BE INSTALLED FACING UP.

STRUCTURAL MEMBERS NAILED TOGETHER FOR ADDED STRENGTH.

IN CARPENTRY TERMS PLATFORM BETWEEN TWO FLIGHTS OF STAIRS TO ALLOW FOR A CHANGE OF DIRECTION.

A BEAM RUNNING HORIZONTALLY ABOVE WINDOW, DOOR, OR OTHER OPENING TO SUPPORT THE STRUCTURAL MEMBERS ABOVE IT.

Definitions 2

RIDGE

PLATE

NONBEARING WALL

RUN

TRIMMER

STRINGER

PETTIBONE

VALLEY

RAFTER

PEAK

PLUMB

ANY WALL WHICH DOES NOT SUPPORT ANY WEIGHT SUCH AS FLOOR FRAMING, ROOF FRAMING, OR CEILING JOISTS.

IN ROOF FRAMING THE HIGHEST POINT OF THE COMMON RAFTERS.

BASICALLY THIS IS JUST A LARGE ROUGH TERRAIN FORKLIFT USED TO MOVE AND ACCESS MATERIAL AROUND MUCH MORE EFFICIENTLY ON THE JOB SITE. THIS MACHINE CAN EASILY BECOME YOUR BEST FRIEND. ESPECIALLY WHEN ROOF FRAMING.

THE TOP AND BOTTOM PLATE IN A WALL.

ON A VERTICAL PLANE, OR UP AND DOWN, AS IN WHEN SOMEONE SAYS "LEVEL THAT WALL" THE CORRECT CARPENTRY TERM IS PLUMB THAT WALL.

THE VARIOUS FRAMING MEMBERS FOR THE ROOF OF A BUILDING.

THE PEAK OR UPPERMOST PORTION OF A SLOPED ROOF.

THE HORIZONTAL DISTANCE COVERED BY ONE STEP, SET OF STEPS, OR A SINGLE RAFTER, NORMALLY HALF THE WIDTH OF THE AREA COVERED BY THE ROOF.

THE MAIN SUPPORT FOR A STAIRCASE, WHICH THE RISERS AND TREADS ARE ATTACHED TO.

THE FRAMING MEMBER NAILED TO THE KING STUD UNDER THE END OF THE HEADER TO SUPPORT THE WEIGHT FROM ABOVE.

WHERE TWO DIFFERENT ROOF SLOPES INTERSECT.

Bible Trivia 1

1. D
2. D
3. D
4. B
5. A
6. A
7. B
8. A
9. D
10. A

Bible Trivia 2

1. C
2. B
3. A
4. B
5. B
6. C
7. A
8. D
9. B
10. D

Bible Trivia 3

1. C
2. A
3. C
4. D
5. C
6. C
7. A
8. B
9. C
10. D

Secret Message 1

Thou hast also given me the shield of thy salvation: and thy gentleness hath made me great.

2 Samuel 22:36

Secret Message 2

The flakes of his flesh are joined together: they are firm in themselves; they cannot be moved.

Job 41:23

Secret Message 3

I know thy works, and charity, and service, and faith, and thy patience, and thy works; and the last to be more than the first.

Revelation 2:19

Secret Message 4

Brethren, if a man be overtaken in a fault, ye which are spiritual, restore such an one in the spirit of meekness; considering thyself, lest thou also be tempted.

Galatians 6:1

Unscramble 1

ACEORGU	COURAGE
DTTTEAUI	ATTITUDE
SPREETC	RESPECT
UVSLAE	VALUES
PGCANITEC	ACCEPTING
ITDADEECD	DEDICATED
WARKHODR	HARDWORK
SRNAMEN	MANNERS
NYIUT	UNITY
HRUTT	TRUTH

Unscramble 2

ALYOLTY	LOYALTY
UUNROSISTID	INDUSTRIOUS
NAGCRI	CARING
VECBLOEENEN	BENEVOLENCE
IIVRGFONG	FORGIVING
SPTLEONIES	POLITENESS
RKOWRE	WORKER
SCMONSOIPA	COMPASSION
THAFLIUF	FAITHFUL
YBVRERA	BRAVERY

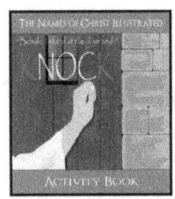

THE NOC ILLUSTRATED
ACTIVITY BOOK

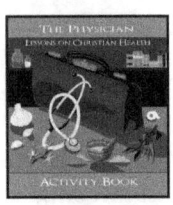

THE PHYSICIAN:
CHRISTIAN HEALTH

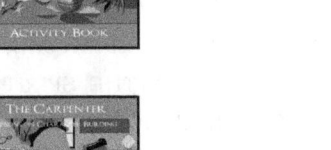

THE CARPENTER:
CHARACTER BUILDING

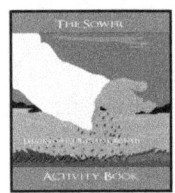

THE SOWER:
CHRISTIAN GROWTH

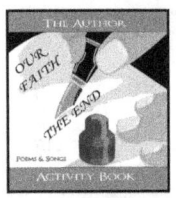

THE AUTHOR:
POEMS & SONGS

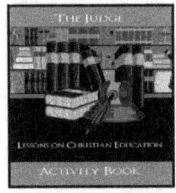

THE JUDGE:
CHRISTIAN EDUCATION

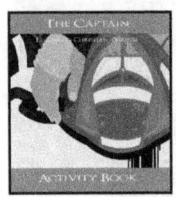

THE CAPTAIN:
CHRISTIAN PURPOSE

"PORTRAITS OF THE SAVIOUR'S
DESIRE TO ENTER HEARTS."

THIS BOOK:

THE CARPENTER

LESSONS ON CHARACTER BUILDING

THE NAMES OF CHRIST ILLUSTRATED

PLEASE VISIT US ONLINE TO VIEW
MORE GREAT TITLES AT:

WWW.THENOCILLUSTRATED.COM